SCAR TISSUE

TRACING MOTHERHOOD

.ll.

SCAR TISSUE

TRACING MOTHERHOOD

SARA DANIÈLE MICHAUD

Translation by **KATIA GRUBISIC**

A Singles essay from LLP

A Singles essay from Linda Leith Publishing, 2023.
Originally published by Éditions Nota bene (a division of Groupe Nota bene), Montreal.
Copyright © 2022, Groupe Nota bene.
Copyright © 2023, Katia Grubisic for the English translation.

Copyedited by Jennifer McMorran, Edward He
Cover image: Berkay08/Adobe Stock
Cover design: Leila Marshy, Debbie Geltner
Book design: DiTech

Library and Archives Canada Cataloguing in Publication

Title: Scar tissue: tracing motherhood/Sara Danièle Michaud; translation by Katia Grubisic.
Other titles: Cicatrices. English
Names: Bélanger Michaud, Sara Danièle, 1980- author. | Grubisic, Katia, translator.
Description: Translation of: Cicatrices, carnets de conversion.
Identifiers: Canadiana (print) 20220425825 | Canadiana (ebook) 20220425841 | ISBN 9781773901374 (softcover) | ISBN 9781773901381 (EPUB) | ISBN 9781773901398 (PDF)
Subjects: LCSH: Bélanger Michaud, Sara Danièle, 1980- | LCSH: Motherhood.
Classification: LCC HQ759 .B4513 2023 | DDC 306.874/3—dc23

Printed and bound in Canada
Legal deposit – Library and Archives Canada and Bibliothèque et Archives nationales du Québec, 2023

The publisher gratefully acknowledges the support of the Government of Canada through the Canada Council for the Arts and the Canada Book Fund.

We acknowledge the financial support of the Government of Canada through the National Translation Program for Book Publishing, an initiative of the Action Plan for Official Languages – 2018–2023: Investing in Our Future, for our translation activities.

We are grateful to the Government of Quebec through the Société du développement culturel and the Programme de crédit d'impôt pour l'édition de livres—Gestion SODEC.

Linda Leith Publishing
Montreal
www.lindaleith.com

To my mother and to my daughter,
for the wildness that binds us.

But does anyone hear me? So I cry out: mama, and I am a daughter and I am a mother. And I have in me the virus of cruel violence and sweetest love.
—Clarice Lispector, *A Breath of Life*

And the I was a mother. The mother. And all my mothers could not save me.
—Rachel Zucker, *MOTHERs*

Two days before I sent her this manuscript to read, my dear friend Mathilde, who lives far away, had a dream: a mother and daughter are on a wooden dock. There is water all around. The daughter bends down. Three pens have been jabbed between the planks. She yanks one out and throws it in the water, then another. The mother pulls out the last pen and hits her daughter with it, knocking her into the water.

***

You don't know this, little one, but for years I've been thinking about the role writing plays in conversion. My mind has been wholly taken up with the question; it suffuses everything I do. I believe writing not only records the process of conversion—it bears witness, it symbolizes—but actually enacts it. Writing about conversion led me to brush up against an experience that was out of my reach, and to not claim it, or no longer, or (please, Christ) never claim it at all. Saints, and especially woman saints, scare me, they exhaust me. Spending too much time with saints drives me toward the profane, to bodily things. Anything to hold the spirit at bay.

I needed to start writing again to escape from you a little, just a little—so little, and with such guilt. I needed to see if my before life was irretrievably lost, sucked in by your starving, smiling, squalling mouth. Yet all I could manage was this notebook, the story of my new, newly scarred, skin. A mother's skin is the marked skin of a converted body, a body that has a new function. A body that needs a new narrative to become habitable.

I'm writing to you out here, out loud, all the words in the open so you won't have to read them, so you don't stumble across handwritten journals someday, my words grabbing you by the throat. Written to you through others, my thoughts and affects, my states of body and mind will vanish with the wind and you will be spared.

You, whom I have to protect from the world and its snake pit of dangers. Maybe it's because I'm getting older, but there seems to be less and less worth saving—just save your own skin, and probably even that will be made into a purse, an old snake-skin bag. Or shed your skin, another relic of conversion.

Above all, I have to protect you from me. I harbour an ancient, unshakeable belief that I wish were unfounded, but which insists on being borne out by my ancestors, one generation after another: a mother of daughters condemns them to being smothered or to running away, or to some tussle between the two, a messy break-dance that only ever circles around the mother. The hope is that, like Persephone, the daughters can get away.

I'm not talking about your grandmother, I'm talking about my mother: she's a different person, one you don't know. And my mother's mother, to whom I sent a photo of you so you'd never have to meet her. To her, you will forever be two-dimensional, a little girl with an eighteen-month-old Mona Lisa smile, and she will be no one to you.

I think I started pulling away from them the day I chose a sort of cowboy look as my everyday uniform—some clothes I fished out of the cedar closet of an old house in the country. Jeans, a white shirt, a leather vest, a woven straw hat, and a skipping rope as a lasso. I see now that my outfit was a suit of armour against women and mothers. For all the good it did me: even if you play dress-up, mothers, and especially your own mother, remain the yardstick of your conversion.

Demeter and Persephone were mother and daughter down to the root: etymologically,

Persephone was initially *Κόρη*, *Kórē*, the maiden, while Demeter, *ἡ Μήτηρ*, *hê Mếtêrή*, means mother. Persephone runs away from her mother by marrying Hades, god of the underworld, and Demeter in turn seeks her out with the single-minded, archetypical, savage determination of a mother who will never give up on her child. A person becomes feral the moment they become a mother: "Savagery in its madness is maternal; it is what makes a mother capable of infanticide, but also of sacrificing her life for her child. It is the obverse of the greatest hatred and of the greatest love. Maternity is the passage from a whisper to the voice that pours a child into the world and holds it, as Salome's voice crafts stories night after night, the thread of rapture without cease, even to the death."[1]

There's a lump in my throat. I wish Demeter had found her daughter, that she had held her in her arms, locking her in her embrace, and not let go. Maybe she should have knocked her out, or drugged her—not to harm her, but to make sure she didn't leave again. What does that say about me, if not that I've undergone a conversion, from being a mother's daughter to a daughter's mother. I am going feral; it's an ambiguous conversion.

No one has articulated that primal tug-of-war, that fatal entanglement between mother and daughter better than the poet Rachel Zucker: "I stepped in. Away from where the body/of my mother is everywhere."[2] Those two lines say it all, and they are not enough, so much that Zucker quotes them, plagiarizing herself and repeating them later in *MOTHERs,* a brutal, extraordinary book that sifts through the sediments of mother–daughter relationships, their appalling harshness, and which ends up killing her mother (literally as well as metaphorically). There's a staggering moment in *MOTHERs* when Zucker, like Persephone, realizes that, although she thought she was running away, she's crashed headlong into her mother:

> Do you understand what I am trying to say? Here are the crib notes: I've been trying to get away from her. Trying to be unlike, alike, unfamiliar, unfamilial. And found all these other mothers but each one was flawed or otherwise human and each one was a lion. And I thought I'd struck out in the other direction, disguised as a peasant, a poet (but not a writer), the mother of sons, not a daughter. And then, when writing about Alice Notley in order to face up to the fact of her influence on my first book,

I saw, years later, that one of Notley's influences was the very book my mother wrote, the very book which I blame, in part, for my parents' divorce, the divorce which I blame in part for my poor relationship with my mother. I had written a book based on a book based on a book written by my mother. Have not gone anywhere. Away from where the body of my mother is everywhere.[3]

It wouldn't have worked. It never does. Even Persephone couldn't make a clean break. She slinks back from Hades six months a year, a snowbird of a girl who cyclically returns to mother and earth.

***

I'm not really going to talk about my mother, even though I'm doing nothing but. I love daughter literature almost as much as I love books about motherhood, and, in any case, they often blur into each other at the vanishing point. Sheila Heti, Adrienne Rich, Rachel Cusk, Rachel Zucker, Maggie Nelson, Alison Bechdel, Sarah Manguso, Elisa Albert, Joan Didion, Anne Dufourmantelle, Fanny Britt, Anaïs Barbeau-Lavalette, Martine Delvaux, Catherine Mavrikakis, in no particular disorder. They are landmarks in my own back-and-forth as a daughter, mother, daughter, mother, daughter, and on and on. Or not landmarks as much as fireflies: fireflies like in that gorgeous picture book *Les lucioles*, Amélie Jackowski's illustrations of Georges Didi-Huberman's reflections. You're only one and a half and you don't understand anything but you ask for that book all the time, your finger tracing the little dots of light shining against the dark pages.

I won't talk about my mother, not really, for two reasons.

The first is a vow: "First psalmodized by a voice," Dufourmantelle writes, "then detached, syllable by syllable, then endowed with speech, the child's body secretly carries vows that bind it to the mother, mortifying or liberating vows that commit both to what neither 'knows' or at least believes they know; what is called destiny."[4]

The vow is bigger than me; it belongs to the realm of psychoanalysis. In *Are You My Mother?*, Alison Bechdel is daring enough to expose her mother and her psyche. I say expose because graphic novels are raw, it's a genre that pulls no punches, especially when the book is a form of psychoanalysis. The representation plays out in images and drawings, all of it coloured by the trivialities and blunders of everyday life: phone conversations that sputter out, therapy sessions where you collapse, dark morning thoughts face-first in a cereal bowl … It is shameless and it is courageous.

I don't want to explain myself to my mother like Bechdel, or kill her like Zucker. If you kill your mother with your words, is that a crime? If a mother dies of a heart attack after reading her daughter's manuscript and trying to convince her not to publish it, is that the same as the daughter stabbing her in the back with a steak knife in the street? I can see myself in that violence, my computer screen suddenly public and the blades of my fingers tapping away the keyboard. As soon as you bring a mother into the story it gets out of hand, everyone knows that. But I'm already too much of a mother to a daughter to attempt matricide.

The second reason is Maggie Nelson, or the indescribable body of the mother, in opposition to Roland Barthes and the infinite mourning for the mother. "A writer is someone who plays with the body of his mother," Nelson writes.

> I am a writer; I must play with the body of my mother. Schuyler does it; Barthes does it; Conrad does it; Ginsberg does it. Why is it so hard for me to do it? For while I've come to see my own body as a mother, and while I can conceive of the bodies of a multitude of strangers as

my mother (basic Buddhist meditation),
I still have a hard time imagining my
mother's body as my mother.[5]

I only touch my mother's body as a formality
or by accident. Since the day it stopped being
mine, there's been no chance for play, I suppose.
Is it a coincidence that the writers Nelson
mentions, who write by, with, and through the
mother's body, are men, sons? Ti-Jean (Kerouac)
and Gabrielle, Allen (Ginsberg) and Naomi,
Roland (Barthes) and Henriette. From one
mother–son pair to another … Maybe they have
nothing in common other than being men. It's
more complicated with Ginsberg, whose mother
was insane and whose insanity he endorsed
as symbolic or even messianic justice. If there
is a common denominator, it is taking the
mother's body as a legitimate sacrifice to which
some connection persists over time, which does
not lead to Hades, even for Ginsberg.

I don't want to play with my mother's body,
which she sacrificed to me and then took back; I
want to be able to beckon that body, which exists
at such a remove and yet from which I sprang, to
think through my own conversion into a mother.
I want to be able to consider motherhood without overly objectifying a mother in a particular
body. I want the outline of a body, a silhouette

glimpsed from afar by nearsighted eyes. I do not want a body I can touch.

***

Of course, I do play with my mother's body.

I thought it might be a matter of common decency, or a crusty loyalty that sabotages my writing or at least drains a lot of material, or else a kind of allegiance, as Dufourmantelle puts it, "against all odds, to her as a likeness, to her, one and only."[6] Yes, but it's not an absolute allegiance; it is more like myopia. I know how my mother's body is defined—small, angular, not swollen at all despite its age, not soft either, and I want to take off my glasses to better summon it into words—to play with it at arm's length. In order to summon the mother, mine and the one that traverses and transcends her, which cuts through her through me to you, my daughter, I need the lines to be blurred. It's not so much a matter of transmission: wildness is an "inheritance without transmission or sharing," an "unbreakable core"[7] you try to break into pieces because it gets stuck, it's impossible to swallow. Transmission is a civilizing force against wildness, it is the best way to make sure our fluids and humours are well behaved, that our blood and tears and our cries are that much more human. But if we lose sight of the outer form of transmission—transmission, which is unique, and every veiled thing it hides—that nearsightedness would reveal a shape like wildness. We would be like beasts that can't understand what they're seeing and just follow the smell of blood, walking blindly into danger. I am that animal.

This is a story of the conversion through which I became a mother, and through which I did not become my mother, or my mother's mother.

> *I stepped in. Away from where the body/of my mother is everywhere.*

"What was her crime?" Zucker asks herself when she realizes that she's run away from her mother only to head straight for her mother; a slap in the face. "And which of her crimes have I not since committed?"[8]

There it is: between the two sides of wildness, the mothers who are daughters of mothers hoard the whole pit for themselves. Some choke on it, but no one spits it out.

Becoming a mother is the most common conversion, the oldest. It's a transformation that absolutely does not involve writing, either upstream or down, and yet I'm writing about it because it's probably the only form of conversion

I've ever experienced—not that I didn't want to, but, like Emil Cioran, I lack that additional necessary devotion.[9] I should have been a mystic. I would have had to become enlightened, a sublimely anachronistic true madwoman of God, or a madwoman of something else, a revolutionary or a heroin addict or something. Framing motherhood as a conversion makes no sense because becoming a mother is such an ordinary, organic conversion, right down to the matter, flesh and mucus, and no matter what story I tell it won't make me more of a mother or a better one. You and your daily needs are what transform me. Motherhood is pure wildness. It's tempting to make it a spiritual thing.

***

You've pulled me out of the books I've had my head in for fifteen years, all those thinkers seeking the sacred, and pushed me to write. But what am I writing? A public notebook, these meandering musings, which might end up being published or else languish encrypted in an old computer that seems to want to roll over and die at every update. Either way, it doesn't matter: even when we write for ourselves, it's public. The moment the words appear on the page or on a screen, any chance at pure immanence is gone. A distance sets in, reflexivity, a dialogue with the self. And there's always a chance the writing will be intercepted, caught by a probing gaze that violates the intimacy of that writing or, conversely, that brings it to life, lets loose a new echo. Spiritual notebooks are public insofar as by not destroying them we abandon them, consciously or not, to a reader, even a single reader, even a bad one.

I would like this notebook to be a way of latching on in a more personal way to the long tradition of the *hypomnèmata,* those ancient spiritual notebooks Michel Foucault talks about in his essay "L'écriture de soi"[10] and whose opinion on conversion pitted him against Pierre Hadot in a sort of friendly intellectual quarrel. I wrote about it, then forgot the essay for six years, then published it suddenly while I was on maternity leave, at a time when the subject of conversion was coming back at me in a way I didn't understand, which I didn't need to understand. What I needed was to think it through, but I had no time in the scant respite from our tyrannical routine, and anyway I don't really know how to talk about these things. I falter and freeze, the sentence dries up before I can get any spit into it and a great profane desert wind sweeps along and carries it away. What spiritual notebooks often solve is a verb-tense problem: if the experience of conversion were as cataclysmic as we think, in an imagination that remains bound to distorted bits of Judeo-Christian tradition, writing about conversion would be tantamount to pastoral care. It never is. It is never Saint Paul struck down, blinded and then transformed, to his very name. In that interpretation, Saint Paul is a victim of conversion. That would be too easy. It's never that simple, even in the canonical texts of saints and mystics who had to burn for their conversion. Saint Augustine—there is nothing more canonical—is a bad convert. He resists, procrastinates, two steps forward and back, stomps around and finally converts—that is, he fashions a conversion narrative. He writes his conversion and in so doing it becomes clear, at least to the reader, that the verb convert doesn't work in the past tense, that every time it's used it works from within to call itself into being, to confer what still resists.

Conversion is always somewhat indistinct, even if our world today could use more of that kind of thing. As we paw through lifestyles to find a way to come back to a supposedly more authentic self, we get bogged down in representations that are usually spectacles, or caricatures. No one knows anyone who struts around, showing off their conversion, or at least nobody would call it a conversion, unless maybe they attend a Pentecostal church or have acquaintances who've converted to an organic vegan gluten-free raw diet (salvation through nutrition: food is the contemporary religion). Getting back to the root of the matter, Hadot reminds us of the etymology of the Latin word *conversio*, which itself refers to two Greek words that mean very different things, almost opposites:

> The Latin word *conversio* in fact corresponds to two Greek words with different meanings, on the one hand *epistrophè*, which means 'change of orientation' and implies the idea of a return (a return to origins, a return to oneself), and on the other hand, *metanoia*, which means 'change of thought' or 'repentance' and implies the idea of mutation and rebirth. Thus, there is in the notion of conversion an internal opposition between the idea of a return to origins and the idea of rebirth.[11]

That dual definition has always bothered me, and I've never known exactly what to do with it other than to tug at the rubber band to see how far we can go in one direction and the other, how we can play on paradoxical ground, how a mutation can coincide with a return to the self. Since we've abandoned any form of religious discourse, we can't avoid all the lifestyle options that seek, directly or indirectly, to improve the individual. We on the secular left stay away from claims of being born again, and from the spectacular, quasi-messianic conversions of revolutionaries. It's much trendier to be on the side of a return to the self and to fall into the aesthetics of existence. That's what Hadot had against Foucault, to some extent, in their discussion of the status warranted or not by ancient spiritual notebooks. All of it is more or less drivel, great speeches that are both comforting and overbearing, sanctimonious snake-oil, life coaching, and pop psychology—what we spout about the sacrosanct return to the self is enough to make you want to cobble together a conversion worthy of a mortificionada like Simone Weil.

The problem with becoming a mother is that you can no longer aspire to be a saint, a madwoman, a revolutionary, someone who rises above or exists on the fringes of filth in a spiritual dialogue cleansed of everything else, because what else matters when you have a direct line to God? You can give up on hygiene, sit on a bed of nails staring at the wall all day without moving, you can let your fingernails grow until they spiral and curl, and it doesn't change a thing. Or you can be someone who is busy smashing the whole fucked up project, amen, through which we roam as we do along the icy streets and slushy sidewalks of our ugly winters—by avoidance. Weaving, winding, avoiding instead of blasting or leaping. Motherhood for me coincided with the return of a bitterness at not having become the revolutionary I aspired to be in my comely college years, when occupying the offices of the Sherbrooke Chamber of Commerce to demand the death of neo-liberalism seemed like a relevant idea, or relevant at least within our blithely, blindly infinite means. I wish I could say that I've revolutionarily sucked the cocks of harried workers like Mathieu Riboulet, but no, I wouldn't have touched that, I'm too much of a snob or a prude. I'm neither a fag (Riboulet), nor a saint (Weil), nor a whore (Nelly Arcan). What's left?

You can't long to be crazy anymore when you become a mother. We know what happens when mothers go mad: they abandon their children, or their children hope they will. To be a mother is a concession to another: you relinquish your self for someone who hasn't really asked for anything and who in receiving develops a taste for asking. You are your child's servant, which is different than being a whore—a submission, a happy mortification in a body that either withers or softens as it ages. Motherhood is not fulfillment, it's just another life, a completely different life than before.

Yet mothers are all a bit mad, a bit cracked. Cracks where the ancient wildness gets in. There's nothing more to say about that damage: there's no way to articulate everything that is torn and rent and what moves inside—come on, a child is the most wonderful gift in the world, we've been at it forever and all the other animals do it too so what's the point of trying to elevate it to a lofty single word, conversion, a word that doesn't mean anything to anyone anymore anyway?

***

It takes place in the body. Yes, it's banal. It's so banal I could scream—scream, moan, spill, split, rip my skin open. It's as ordinary as childbirth, but birth is only one part of the mutation. I'm fascinated by the place of the body in Riboulet's work, notably in *Entre les deux, il n'y a rien*; by sex and by revolution, which is nothing more than conversion exiting the body, conversion taking place elsewhere, taking up all the bodies in one movement. You have to be in your body to be able to give it, and the body is already full of endless imparting; the transmission never stops, running through the veins and seeping from the pores. It's a game of filling and emptying, and books are the trough and the dumping ground, where we seek nourishment and where we unload, where we call to God or any other force in or beyond this world.

"It leaves the books and comes into the body," Riboulet writes, "and to have peace it must again leave in the books,"[12] back and forth. If it were true, if it didn't have to be shoved into truth … Or maybe it is true, but all truths must be made true; you have to write, you have to boast about it, you have to get stuck, you have to make sure that there is no possible return. That's why converts write all the time, whether the turn is right side up or upside down (and the Oscar goes to Emmanuel Carrère, for his sublime confession: those who have converted and deconverted have gone through everything). You have to leave a mark, show that you've been there: get out your spray paint and tag a chunk of stone, an edge of wall, a piece of paper. Etch yourself into space–time for history and posterity. But it's an obligatory journey too, because writing continues the experience of conversion itself, that is to say, writing prolongs it, it performs the conversion, and even chases it down in a sense because it's too big, too fast, too extraordinary and at once so ordinary, too humbly biological (in the case of motherhood, and maybe only for mother-hood). We need writing and all the apparatus of knowledge and gesture it summons in order to acknowledge the shock of conversion, and to come to terms with it.

And now you're asleep and I've forgotten about you even though it's you I'm talking to. You've been sleeping for hours and I can't let you sleep any longer, you've clambered into my brain again, not even figuratively but in my flesh, with your smiles, your tears, how we cling to each other … You, to whom I am writing out here, out loud, so that you won't have to read my words someday.

***

I wish I could adapt, recalibrate, just tune up or down, get the pitch right. I go from you to writing, trying to skip over what's less important, and what takes up most of my time. I don't even know what I'm tuning into or out of anymore. It's grammatical again: the agreement is backward, the subject agreeing with the verb rather than the other way around. I am so often paralyzed by anxious inertia; I am made of stone. I can't make a single sound, never mind a whole tune. How can a stone be expected to resound, to echo? A stone doesn't sing; it is moved, thrown, blown up. Most of the time it just sits there, wondering what the hell is going on.

The last time I moved house, I came across a picture. It's early fall, I must have been fourteen or fifteen months old. I'm sitting in the grass near our cottage, which I still remember as a lost paradise. I'm all baby fat, and dressed in a getup so typical of the eighties, the little overalls and the gender-neutral colours, the woolly jacket, a striped hat and matching knee socks. The photo captures the full expression of my mineral self: grounded, in the grass, without the least intention of moving from my limited perimeter. The photo is less a portrait of me than a scene I happen to be in. My father's in the shot too, in the upper right corner, standing in the bed of his reddish-orange pickup truck, long beard, wool socks and Adidas sneakers—his signature four-season style at the time—unloading firewood. I'm not looking in his direction, just letting him work. My world is enormous, and I don't have to be in tune with anything in particular. I wasn't a demanding child, according to family lore. They called me wise—the wisdom of the stones, which ask for nothing, nothing but a place somewhere in the grass.

***

"He is the baby unchaotic/he is born and I am undone—feel as if I will/never be, was never born," Alice Notley writes in her poem "A Baby is Born Out of a White Owl's Forehead"; "Two years later I obliterate myself again/having a second child/[…] for two years, there's no me here."[13] Soon you'll be two and I'm still not here, still not where I thought I used to be, where I was never properly embodied, too brittle a stone in the middle of that vast landscape. That photo of me with my father by the woodpile is the impossibility of going back to the beginning, it's a nostalgia for something I don't remember. Conversion vertigo. Maintaining an imaginary relationship with childhood is required in order to cross over to the other side, the side of wildness, to step into the transmission of a much, much older memory, of a before-world that's out of reach once the conversion is complete. The conversion is into a body, and that body knows—what an outrageous dissociation, converted first by the body, converted to such a love, the plot of which has been written billions of times before and which will be rewritten again and again, with all the ambiguity of the sacred. The affective experience of the sacred is necessarily formulated in ambiguity. Rudolf Otto speaks of it as a *mysterium fascinans* and a *mysterium tremendum*,[14] between fascination and terror, rapture and fear. In motherhood, the sacred puts me at the junction between care in the most absolute sense, a form of everyday devotion, awash in milk, tears, drool, and mustard-yellow shit, all the fluids that are conductors of love, and then the ever-present aggression dangling off devotion's nose, a tipping point, inevitable. It's part of the wildness, the moment when it first erupts and you realize that you've crossed over. A mother is one who fails, one who has failed, one who will fail. When I was pregnant, I read Donald Winnicott on the good-enough mother,[15] the mother who is merely ordinarily devoted. I enjoyed the bracing mediocrity of the idea, into which I projected myself completely, but it's bunk, just a nice idea, perfect and composed and devoid of wildness. It is a man's idea. A mother is never good enough or else she is too good, she is suffocating, she has no boundaries, there is no distinction between one self and the other. The relationship is forced—at first, it's too much, then not enough because she's tired of being bound to the needs of a tiny dictator, and then again too much in order to compensate, because of the guilt—the guilt I wouldn't even want to let go of, because without that, imagine … I yell at you in the middle of the night when you don't want to sleep, I can't understand what you want. It's late, I want to sleep, we're in the middle of a move, I'm at the end of my rope, I want to sleep, do you understand, I want you to be quiet, I want you to be quiet on your own, without me having to take care of you, I don't have the strength left to hold you gently, do you understand, if I pick you up it's going to be rough, maybe on purpose to shake you up a little and then I'll feel bad, but you're whining and wailing and fine I'll pick you up, see, it's rough, believe me, there's not much love in it, and I wonder was I glad that you were crying to so I could grab you like that, give in to aggression, feeding off it, though just a little, so little, because, fortunately, it never goes too far. I'm not calming you down but I'm not making it worse either. Thankfully you're not very sensitive to my mood swings, you understand already that your mother is a little bit cracked and that it's better to rely on your father's constancy. He's never too much and never not enough. I know it's in bad faith to say that, on your behalf or mine, but it's the same thing: if supper is late when he's in charge, magically there is no drama and he never has to do it all with one hand while balancing you on his hip with the other, squirming and impatient. I like the good Doctor Winnicott, but it really is such a man's idea, the good-enough mother. How could you go from wild to good enough without losing yourself, stripping yourself of your violent love, one skin cell at a time? Mind you, it might be nice to break with the standards and the compartmentalization, the immemorial archetypes that have been activating the unconscious since the dawn of time; another conversion. But I am desperately, wildly, lovingly a mother, and that night, when your father got home, I handed you over and went to curl up in bed with my guilt. He didn't judge me, but he didn't absolve me of my well-earned remorse either. The verdict: not good enough. And then, of course, I attributed your marked preference for your father in the weeks that followed to that night, that falling-out between us: I let you down, I wasn't good enough, there was no excuse. Being at the end of my rope is no excuse, I shouldn't have let things get that far, it was my problem. "I understand that I am alone with my outburst," Rachel Cusk writes, "that I myself have moved outside the shelter of love. As a mother I do not exist within the forgiving context of another person. I realise that this is what being in charge is."[16]

One day I stopped being hungry, I couldn't say yes to anything or anyone, I was slumped in my bed, feverish and shivering, in tears. The thing that took control wasn't just a virus, or maybe it had been conjured on purpose so that I could stop, so it would finally be over. That day, I would have liked to not be in charge. The little girl in me exists only in order to need, and for that need to remain, inarticulate, whole, and unfulfilled, so that the mother remembers what it's like to wake up crying all alone in the night, at least sometimes.

***

The minor dramas of our day-to-day are a world away from the expansive, uneven, continuous pulse of our bond. Like a mystic, I tell the story of grace and acedia, especially the latter. I find acedia, that listlessness or torpor, an unconcern with the self in the world, more affecting than grace. I am profane, I cannot imagine infallible love; even the love I have for you, the fullest I have ever known, has gaps and blind spots. Mystics swing back and forth between nothingness and everything-ness, but even that doesn't transpose to the belly. You, inside me or out—I was no fuller or emptier before, you just borrowed my body, we cohabited but were never one, as much as I would have loved that. I've always both fallen short of fusion and sought it, hence my fascination for mystics, but that's not how it works. Even my flesh had to be sliced open to get to you. As far as departures go, you left rather abruptly. And then the morphine and the swollen, empty belly, all stitched up, pain, and there was you I had no idea what to do with. In those first photos I look like I know what I'm doing, but trust me, it's all a lie. The Madonna and child pose was for show.

My body, my terms, more or less: I didn't drink, I ate what the gestational diabetes allowed, but I kept running, rocking you as I ran. I ran and you matched my rhythm. I never stopped. I wasn't the kind of pregnant person to sit around placidly and rub my belly. Outside of my body, meanwhile, we're clearly on your terms. Where and when did the conversion begin exactly? The belly is such a strong symbol: the cut, the scar, the sign that nothing will ever be the same. I try to map what I went through onto the mystical experience, the full and the empty, but what I understand above all is the emptiness, the abyss, what remains after a state of grace that is only ever temporary. The envelope of skin contains nothing, a husk of dried-up spirit that no longer knows how to think of itself. That may be the heart of our drama: for a few minutes, I was scared that I would lose you before getting to hold you in my arms, I had to be cut open because my body could no longer sustain you and instead was holding you prisoner. That scar, what it left on my already and still-fragile mind. Even now, years later, it comes up out of nowhere, more and more often—while I'm picking you up at daycare, when I'm marking papers, at the grocery store. I put myself through other, imaginary dramas. This week I dreamt three times that we were taken to a concentration camp. I was holding back tears as I explained that we would be separated, your father and you and I. It wasn't just a nightmare, it's the nightmarish reality of what I'm afraid of, a fist of anxiety lurking at every turn, every thought. It pops up and I can't breathe, the fear is the most vivid thing. I'm afraid of this world in which if we were any wiser we wouldn't dare give birth. The world reeks of apocalypse, it's impossible to ignore. I'm afraid of being taken away from you. I'm afraid of not being able to protect you, though I'm not really sure from whom or what. From shapeless perils you'll probably never face? The world going dark? From evil, or just pain? From others, that eternal source of aggression? From me, the ambiguous mother, never good enough but never completely inadequate, straddling good and evil as if I had any right? Rachel Cusk writes about waking up to the same fear for a long time:

> As time passes, I grow more and more tormented by the idea of children being unloved. My heart clinches at stories of

abandonment and abuse. I weep before pictures on the news of orphans, refugees, children of war. A weekly television programme devoted to children having operations causes me to tear at the sofa with frantic nails. My compassion, my generalised human pity, has become concentrated into a single wound, a dark sore of knowing and of the ability to inflict. I realize that in love I have always considered myself to be victim rather than aggressor, that I have cherished a belief in my own innocence, in what nevertheless I have styled as a conflict, an irreconcilable struggle. Like a state benefit, love has always seemed to me to be something to which people have inalienable rights, a belief that there is a mirror mask for my terror at the possibility of being unloved. [...] It seems that it is not to love but to us like that I am suddenly alive. I have not, in fact, become more loving, more generous, more capacious. I have merely become more afraid of love's limits, and more certain that they exist.[17]

I'm down in the ring with you, deep underground—a prefab, spiderwebby basement with an antique washer growling from having one too many loads of diapers crammed in. We'll see who makes the first move, who throws the first punch, though I'll be the one to end the fight with a hug. And you will inevitably pull away.

I know the line between victim and perpetrator is never as clear as we'd like. And, really, I wasn't a victim of anything. Neither were you. Where does that reflex come from, to identify with the victim? Is it a typically female impulse? (And by typically, naturally I mean constructed, created, imposed.) It harks back to my previous life, and it has shifted in the conversion to motherhood: we begin to identify with the bad guy, and we can't cry over the victims anymore—the hypostasis of babies into victims—and we sink into a muddy, subterranean consciousness, its incredible opacity, an awareness that love has so many opponents and that it can be defeated. That's what's terrifying. Sometimes the existence of love is insufficient. We try to count it: what is the amount of love? If I love you a thousand times a hundred minus twelve, how much does that work out to? Are instances of slight neglect subtracted from the sum of care?

***

In *The Writing Life*, an essay on writing, on the how of writing, its modalities and requirements, Annie Dillard revisits Thoreau's extended meta- phor about the bee and the honey tree, about how a book guides its own author: the bee leads to the honey tree. She takes it up as a sounding board for another metaphor—cruder, meaty, more wildly maternal:

> You may be wondering how to make the first move, how to catch the first bee. What bait to use. You have no choice. One bad winter in the Arctic, and not too long ago, an Algonquin woman and her baby were left alone after everyone else in their camp had starved. Ernest Thompson Seton tells it. The woman walked from the camp where everyone had died, and found at a lake a cache. The cache contained one small fish-hook. It was simple to rig a line, but she had no bait, and no hope of bait. The baby cried. She took a knife and cut a strip from her own thigh. She fished with the worm of her own flesh and caught a jackfish; she fed the child and herself. Of course she saved the fish gut for bait. She lived alone at the lake, on fish, until spring, when she walked out again and found people. Seton's informant had seen the scar on her thigh.[18]

Winnie the Pooh could never have been an Indigenous invention; nor could Annie Dillard have made him up.

Nobody writes because they have something to say. Having something to say is totally secondary. Whether it's deep or not, some random thought, when we have something to say, we say it, out in the air, or over a beer, or on one platform or another. There's always an audience for those who have something to say (attending comedy school is even better; being funny, in Québec at least, is a sign of depth). There's no need to slather countless pages that nobody will read—almost nobody, and especially not you, I hope. Sometimes we write because we have something to hide and we beat around the bush endlessly, book upon book, but we end up spilling the beans, a few at a time or all at once. Or we write because there's something missing, and there's nothing to hide except the fact that something is missing. We write out of hunger, a spiritual hunger that no food, no everyday delight, nothing that has been written before can satisfy. The ultimate allegory of writing is Knut Hamsun's *Hunger*[19]: writing in order to earn enough to buy a piece of bread and then not being able to write anymore, filled and stilled as soon as you're satisfied by a spiritual emptiness. In my case, it's literal. I'm invariably hungry when I'm writing. I stoke my hunger, I tend it. With apologies to Thoreau, I'm not looking for anything to spread on my toast, and anyway there's nothing sweet about this kind of hunger. I do not crave the taste of honey. This is a hunger for something alive and raw and fleshy, a hunger for what sticks to the ribs and will sustain me enough to feed you. It's not just me, I'm not just chasing bees for fun, for a bit of honey, and what's a sting or two? You are with me and it's you who is hungry, you are the one with needs, and I have to give you what I don't have, what I'm looking for myself, what I am hungry for, which is elsewhere, in words unread, words unwritten. The bait is my own flesh—you can't catch anything with a bare lure, you need a bit of blood on the hook, and writing isn't bare or transparent either, it's a projection of the mind that is caught by the cuts in the flesh, those pieces of yourself you offer up because you have nothing else to write with and you're hungry for something that can't be written.

***

I love Thomas Bernhard's obsessive, cerebral characters, ruminants of hypothetical writing. One of them, Konrad, in *The Lime Works*, plans a treatise for years, crafting it all in his head, down to the last detail, but he never manages to write down a single word. His life is summed up by his inability to tip his head over and "empty out its contents."[20] The image of the mind as a trash can that pours out and spills words onto paper delights me, probably because it feels so foreign. What a sadly masturbatory, phallic image of the mind that can't come, that can't produce anything concrete or external. Write outside of the self. Dump out your mind, like garbage, onto paper. Or not: write inward. Draw a line of words, then another inside it. Maybe it will fill something.

I am writing out loud so you don't have to read me someday. I am writing to the inside of us. Fishing with flesh and catching scars. Until they fade, all the way back to the heart. The scar on my belly looks like a tentative smile. For a long time, it disgusted me, scared me. I didn't want to touch it, brush against it, think about it. Flesh sliced open is such an ordinary thing, but the pain was real, and the scar is too. I was cut open so you could come out of me, so you could live. It's the same story, always the same, and yet I never would have thought that my scar, a mark at once so deeply intimate and utterly alien, could become literary. Literally literary. A scar, a mother, writing. A mother, the writing, the scar. Writing, scarring, mothering. Scar, write, mother. What's the order supposed to be? The order of the words changes their meaning. In one universe, the scar made the mother, the mother makes the writing, and therefore the scar is necessary for the writing. Linear, logical, reassuring. That's how it's supposed to go. Start with the chicken, start with the egg, one or the other, but as long as you start somewhere you'll have chicken and eggs to eat. Writing, however, does not exist to create an objective account, within the self or beyond. You don't have to explain everything—what a pain in the ass that would be, it's not like death, though death is anything but tedious. Tedious is shopping for baby stuff at Walmart, hating yourself for being reduced to that, wanting to die. Writing is not about expressing, about getting it out, but rather about inscribing, within the self— "the line of words fingers your own heart,"[21] as Dillard puts it. You fish with your own flesh, you work out your own scar, a scar that forms inside the text. There's nothing reassuring about it: writing as scarring. In this universe, writing predates the scar, and the mother too; the mother and the words are the ones making the scar. The chicken and the egg exist only for each other and know nothing of anything else. For a few days it's been just me and Clarice, and through Lispector I am able to stop asking why I write; she has pondered the metaphysics of that coop better than anyone.

As for which came first, it was the egg that found the chicken. The chicken was not even summoned. The chicken is directly singled out. — The chicken lives as if in a dream. She has no sense of reality. All the chicken's fright comes because they're always interrupting her reverie. The chicken is a sound sleep. — The chicken suffers from an unknown ailment. The chicken's unknown ailment is the egg. — She doesn't know how to explain herself: 'I know that the error is inside me', she calls her life an error.[22]

The chicken is blind and vapid, blissfully unaware, and prefers the evanescence of day-dreams to the abstract weight of the egg within, yet the chicken has been chosen by the egg. I think the egg is the sacred, an unspeakable density we live with and without which we cannot live, it's everything there is to say and hide and everything that has never been said and hidden, it must be named absolutely and no matter the cost, and hidden jealously, modestly, foolishly, it's not a matter of expressing content, it has nothing to do with that, and in any case, the more you say, the more you hide. You speak, you write, "and the egg is fully protected by all those words."[23] Writing a book is not like laying an egg; it doesn't just come out fully formed. You can't let go of that egg, and I guess that's where the wildness of motherhood and the wildness of writing converge, though what happens in that juncture is tucked away inside the shell, and if it breaks it no longer exists. "An egg is a thing that must be careful," Lispector writes. "That's why the chicken is the egg in disguise. The chicken exists so that the egg can traverse the ages. That's what a mother is for."[24]

There are so many ways to get tangled up in knots of inextricable metaphors. I'm not sure if we're going to figure it out this time; the egg-white mucus of writing is thick and sticky. Clarice never looked for a way out; I think she never needed to. She wove her web, staying there, chatting with whatever insect got stuck. Trying to explain my way out must be an academic instinct—explaining, and especially watching myself explain. But I'm not really standing outside the web. I am the insect. The spider has disappeared, and it's up to me to weave the rest, knit, purl, as best I can: scar, writing, mother, one row and the next, an inseparable trinity, and I don't know what thread to pull to start untangling.

***

The mother sprang into existence because you did, softly first, a tiny pearl of delicate life in a shell of cells, then louder, screaming and raw, without the second coddling of skin. You exist in all the ways you can, and I am irremediably a mother. But I am not writing my conversion to motherhood. It would be too straightforward for me to star in this version of the story. No, I am a mother because I write. By tracing the scar and seeing where it goes in a conversion notebook, that's how the mother exists. There was a cut, then you, and the scar that remains is only superficial, it's anchored in the skin but not really attached to anything else. It's tenuous, and maybe that's why it has to be carved out again and again, stitched up, written.

***

Have I found my actual subject? The nucleus, the heart, the egg. I would probably just break it immediately if I had it in my hands, gratuitously, without even making an omelette, and no way to hide the mess. "The chicken must not know she has an egg"; Lispector again. "Or else she would save herself of the chicken, which is no guarantee either, but she would lose the egg. So she doesn't know."[25] So I don't know. When I suggest that I am not in fact writing my conversion into motherhood, in spite of appearances, that the opposite is true, that I am a mother because I write … Am I speaking or fleeing? Is this about Demeter or Persephone? Are you slipping away from me so fast that I have to create you? Or have I found the best and dumbest way to lose you for good?

So many questions are tumbling out, and what I really want to do is consult the oracle, like Sheila Heti in *Motherhood*. That book too is a kind of public notebook, in which Heti asks herself the big motherhood question—does she want to, it is possible, is it not, the constraints, the sacrifices—for herself and for every woman before and after who has been free to choose, who does and who will. You can't always be alone with your questions, or rather, in fact, it's possible to be terrible at being alone with your questions, or to be terribly alone with your questions, until they coalesce into a barricade against thinking at all, until you feel like you have to project yourself into dialogue with tran-scendence. Like Jacob, she is wrestling with an angel, with an unknown: "Whether I want kids is a secret I keep from myself—it is the greatest secret I keep from myself."[26] She keeps asking the I Ching (although it's still a game of yes or no, she tries to get around that by asking increas-ingly complex questions), and the pithy answers she gets do seem to satisfy her momentarily, allowing her to come at the question a differ-ent way; and they annoy her, they show her that she's just going around in circles, that divination is pointless and that a mere game will never make up for faithlessness. Still, she can't discard the I Ching, the oracular function of which has been displaced by its role as a literary device. Is there any difference? Writing is thought made manifest, a textual framework scaffolded with a throw of the dice. "In this book," Heti makes a point of prefacing, "all results from the flipping of coins result from the flipping of actual coins,"[27] literalizing what the literary object has spiritually put into play. Writing itself becomes a throw of the dice, and the I Ching is just an allegory of writing.

> I know the longer I work on this book, the less likely it is I will have a child. Maybe that is why I'm writing it—to get myself to the other shore, childless and alone. This book is a boundary I am erecting between myself and the reality of a child. Perhaps what I'm trying to do in writing this is build a raft that will carry me just so long and so far, that my questions can no longer be asked. This book is a life raft to get me there. For myself, that's all it needs to be— not a great big ocean liner, just a barge. It can completely fall to pieces once I land on the other shore.[28]

Writing is not the vessel of questions and thoughts but their vehicle, without which they would just stomp around, going nowhere. Heti's answer didn't come with the sharpness of a blade slicing down. She wrestled with it like Jacob with the angel, in the writing itself, until the book was done, the river crossed. The writing will beget the child, or it will beget the unborn child, the child never to be born. "Writing seems so small in comparison to motherhood. It doesn't feel like it will fill up all the nooks and crannies of the soul. And perhaps it won't. But even if one is a mother, are all the nooks and crannies filled up?"[29]

She hems and haws and she has no choice but to come up with a third option. Of writing and motherhood, which would be the most likely or the least to fill up all the hidden corners of the soul, the spirit? Her own mother admits that, in her case, motherhood was not fulfillment. "Right before my mother left the room, she spoke, with some confusion, about women who say that raising kids is the most important thing in their life. I asked her if motherhood had been the most important part of her life, and she blushed and said, *No*—at the very same moment that I interrupted her and said, *You don't have to answer. I was there.*"[30]

Their responses overlap and converge, not so much in the conversations between them, but in the short-circuit of the book—an object created from a thought that carries within it an implied wager, a necessary blind spot perhaps, or half-conscious, subconscious, that writing would be able to make up for something, fill those nooks and crannies.

But does writing fill and fulfill? I can't argue with Heti's extraordinary faith in writing, a faith her doubts only begin to scratch the surface of, though in truth they don't leave much of a mark at all. All I can do is cite her own words, which seems underhanded, making her say what she isn't saying, what writing and her writing are hiding, or what I think they're hiding. *You don't have to answer. I am here.*

The book is called *Motherhood,* but in my head I rename it *Daughterhood*. When we read, we wield the power to rename, repeat, retell, repeal, expand, distort. This book of Heti's covers her last fertile years, those few critical moments before the best-before; forty is imposing precisely because it feels like an expiry date. The book is about a girl who wonders if she wants to, can, and will become a mother, but more than that it's a space where she discovers a more indelible identity: "I was a daughter—*existentially*—and I always would be."[31] As her mother was and is too, which suggests that motherhood and daughterhood are not mutually exclusive. What's growing in the daughter's belly is writing (for her; for her mother, it's work), which has to be able to fill the fissures and breaches, the secret recesses, the injustices, the parts of the story gone wrong, the parts where life goes wrong, and especially it has to be able to dry her mother's tears.

Once upon a time, there was writing and there was a daughter. Once upon a time, we, daughters who did not satisfy our mothers, we daughters converted into writers. All the tears of our mothers were left untouched by our powerless hands, which take on both the wavering power and the impotence of words to even try. Trying to be able to: maybe that's the definition for this genre, the public notebook *au féminin*, the essays I'm sipping from, which I'm drunk on. Upholding the ideal that writing is able to try, that the daughter, through writing, is able to save her mother (Heti), or kill her mother (Zucker), or ignore her (me).

Diane Wolkstein, Rachel Zucker's mother, told her, "the power of language and stories … was remarkable … and more beautiful than anything that was in my life."[32] The superlative is enough to drive a daughter to matricide.

"I stepped in away from where the body of my mother was everywhere," the litany that Zucker repeats, from *Eating in the Underworld* to *MOTHERs,* takes on another resonance here. Writing about motherhood brings us back to the first experience, of being a daughter, which can never be outdone or outgrown. The mother's body in the daughter who becomes a mother, the mother's presence in the space (the writing) she chooses in order to escape and which her mother also chose to escape from her ... All of these books are so full of subtitles, or anti-titles perhaps. They are obvious everywhere in the text. Motherhood achieved or announced, desired or feared, is first and foremost daughter-hood. No word quite exists to describe the condition, but the neologism is clear. At first, you are the centre of her world and the locus of imperious need, then daughter, as the body is pried away from the source of its satisfaction, daughter of a mother, a mother who fulfills or doesn't, and who isn't fulfilled either ... And then what? Mother, or not, mother/writer, childless writer?

Daughters, mothers, writers, all of us are lumped into the same pile, to insert fullness into lack when the emptiness takes up too much room. Fulfill: full, fill, all the combinations and permutations are possible—even, surely, negation.

And if a daughter admits that she has fallen short of fulfilling her mother, that she hasn't been able to fix her mother, in real life and in writing, can she give birth to the mother? If she's given up on even trying to fix her, can she give birth to the writer? This is not a metaphor; I don't mean becoming or metamorphosis. Giving birth is something else entirely. When you give birth, you become twofold, you have to think and live for two, and at the same time you have to coexist, live alongside, think alongside, resist the temptation to swallow the other and also resist the temptation to just exist as continuous scarification, healing over the other until you are nothing but scars upon scars. Is that the conversion I want to talk about? It's not exactly epistrophe (a return—to origins, to the self), nor quite metanoia (rebirth), but giving birth. Not transformation but cleaving. I can't see what it means yet, let alone where it will lead me.

***

Is this the book in which the defective daughter gives birth to the mother? Am I supposed to write in spite of that deficiency? Or because of it? Is it possible to give birth simultaneously to the mother and to the writer? This line of questioning is beyond me, *pace* Socrates, but I can feel it working from within, like a contraction. Dare I compare …? No, it's not that violent, and there isn't the possibility of death lurking down the hall. Is this a book in which a mother is born, or a child in which a writer is born? That's a bit odd: the writer born of the child. The child is not a space, though I guess the book isn't either. Or maybe they are after all, both so magnetic, physically and spiritually. I am mobilized and immobilized at once, I am contained in territories I barely know and over which I have no dominion.

You are turning me into a writer through the need I have to escape from you for hours into a cell that I wish were hermetic so that I could belong to you wholly afterward, and then unbelong once more. I'm only able to belong to you at intervals. You cannot fulfill me, though admitting that hurts, but it's not your job and never will be. And even if one day you decide to write like me, that won't be for fulfillment either. You exist for something else, to discover the world and to love it, to land here like sunbeams and silliness. Your wild golden curls hold that already. Not to make me whole.

And know that if I had to choose between you and writing, if I were forced to choose, it wouldn't be impossible at all, not in the least. Always you. I would never be able to lose you. It's absurd to try to fathom that kind of choice. Maybe I'm thinking of it at all because of a game we used to play with my sister, a ridiculous competition between equally unpalatable options: would you rather sleep with James Franco, only covered in pus and boils, or wash Donald Trump's feet with your tongue, that sort of thing. Writing or you? You, you. You I never want to stop holding, you in whom my life is folded, until the end of time, you. "Heat drawn from the well of devotion that is the female heart,"[33] as Patti Smith writes. Yet I persist, writing and writing to you for all the world to see so that you don't have to read me someday. I write to sanctify each day with you, days I would otherwise debase.

***

Heti made the choice I didn't. I am thirty-nine years old; seventy-one in nostalgia years and about twenty-two in maturity. I'm running full tilt at my best-before. I had you. I have you.

I've just turned thirty-nine and I'm freaking out that I might be pregnant again. I bought a test I'm waiting to take. I got the one that tells you six days before your period is due. One little drip of urine and I could find out right now, but

I don't. I need a panic interlude, I need to run off my anxiety, cry, think. Maybe writing down my fear led to genesis. I'm crazy enough to believe that writing brings about reality. How ludicrous it would be to create something I don't want. I wanted you, completely, absolutely, and I never want to want anything that much again. Except I didn't know that I didn't want it before this scare, and now it might be too late. Surely by the age of thirty-nine you might expect to know what you want without getting all tragic about it. I'm working on my powerlessness. I probe the end of it and the outline, I suck around in the mucky bottom. This is just a sidebar, a bottomless pit where everything is possible and therefore impossible, and it might already be out of my control. Is there something or is there nothing? Is it even possible that there would still be nothing, since it exists in the writing? Just a few more hours, though they may become days: I need to stretch out my worry, blow it out like a bubble and lose my mind before it pops in my face, with a positive I don't want or a negative that maybe I don't want either, because I've spent so long imagining the worst.

***

"*Are you going to have a child? If I do, I do—and if not, not.*"[34] If not, not: Heti borrows the phrase from the oligarchs in Barcelona's Council of One Hundred, who swore an oath to the king: "*We, who are as good as you, swear to you, who are no better than us, to accept you as our king and sovereign, provided you observe all of our liberties and laws—but if not, not.*"[35]

Those three words have such heft. If not, not. There may be no more efficient formula to combine possibility and resistance in an absolutely vague way—it's assertively vague, it speaks volumes and it is also a negation. It does not reveal, nor hide.

> *Are you going to have a child? If I do, I do—and if not, not.* […] and I don't want 'not a mother' to be part of who I am—for my identity to be the negative of someone else's positive identity. Then maybe instead of being 'not a mother' I could be not *'not a mother'*. I could be *not not*.
>
> The negative cancels out the negative and I simply am. I am what I positively am, for the *not* before the *not* shields me from being simply *not* a mother. And to those who would say, *You're not a mother*, I would reply, 'In fact, I am not not a mother.' […]

Yet someone who is called a mother could also say, 'In fact, I am not not a mother.' Which means she is a mother, for the *not* cancels out the *not*. To be *not not* as what the mothers can be, and what the women who are not mothers can be. This is the term we can share. In this way, we can be the same.[36]

The double negative acts as armour for all those who are also not what they are. Deep down, who is completely what she is, without any doubt, without ever wanting to back out or change her mind? *I am not not a mother.* What I am not is full of possibilities, and what I am no longer, and what I am. The resistance to and of self-definition is contained in the same phrase, mathematical, paradoxical, and terribly efficient. Probably it's completely normal that I would get to this point in wanting to try to write a conversion notebook. There's a bit of self-sabotage required in writing; it keeps things exciting. But this is not literally artifice; artificiality does not exist in my paranoid world, where everything means something, though half the time I don't understand what. The only thing that keeps me from being locked up is that I don't understand the signified of which all things and all events are signs. Conversion is for saints and madwomen. I mean serious conversions, because everyone's constantly converting to one thing or another: yoga, jogging, organic food, sugar-free diet, gluten free, dry Januaries, kale and grasshopper powder smoothies. Contemporary conversion must first target the body and then produce some kind of spiritual transfiguration, not as a rebound effect but as the telltale sign of our collective bullshit, which only reinforces the pressure I feel to do the same. I converted to running many years ago. I run fairly often, and I'm fast, according to my smartwatch and my partner, but I'm still just as cracked, though not crazy. There's nothing more irritating than people who claim that their particular madness is something special. I'm not crazy, I'm not special. Just a little cracked, like your favourite mug, dropped one too many times on its way out of the dishwasher and chipped right where you usually put your mouth, on the other side of the cup's handle. I'm chipped. No matter how fast I run, it doesn't unbreak me, it won't make me whole again.

I no longer know where reality and literature overlap. Where does that ambivalence come from? My eternal second-guessing? All the conversion narratives I've absorbed over the years are deep wells of doubt—crushing, sometimes. It may be that conversion as a mode hinges on doubt, maybe converting is all about doubting so much that the status quo becomes unbearable, until life or time decides for you, as it does for Heti. But conversion narratives are also a literary genre, with its own set of codes. Maybe they come from the *Confessions* of Saint Augustine, the master. I remember something about a long, profound hesitation prior to the revelation among the olive trees, where the oracle is revealed in the sacred book, where he makes of the book an oracle. Serendipitously, I found the passage right away in my recent edition of the oft-translated *Confessions*; the book fell open to the right place, the spine broken there by magic. Augustine is at his best in that expression of inner conflict, I find. He can't quite go over to the other side, the duelling wills come up against each other and he is undone:

> A new will had begun to emerge in me, the will to worship you disinterestedly and enjoy you, O God, our only sure felicity; but it was not capable of surmounting that earlier will strengthened by inveterate custom. And saw the two wheels folded out— the old and the new, the one carnal, the

other spiritual—and in their struggle tore my soul apart.[37]

Daughter, you are the sacred in my life and yet so often I can't do it and I don't even know what it is that I can't do, that pronoun contains and conceals everything and maybe I need some measure of transcendence to be able to break through. As if there were nothing of conversion in the predictability of immanence without resorting to the same old outdated categories.

***

Stand on the threshold, on the pass line, where you could tip, where you don't know if you want to walk the tightrope or free fall. I have fallen to the other side of the conversion line, the other side of where I always was. I persist in reaching out to touch the glass that separates me from the past, from the life in which I was just me and it took everything I had. If I had a second child, I think I wouldn't even be able to touch the glass, I would be pulled into a motherhood not only with no return but also without room for nostalgic contemplation.

My favourite sport is nostalgia. I have a nostalgic soul; I should have been born Portuguese or Romanian so I could have had words for countless shades of nostalgia. I burnish the past in my head, I erase its sharp edges, I am nostalgic for moments that objectively deserve no nostalgia. I am nostalgic for my nostalgia. I anoint the present with the past and dream of a future from which both have been excised. I am in dire need of a second chance, the kind of existential leap Kierkegaard talks about[38]: the second degree of consciousness that repetition enables, a kind of transposed repetition where the same landscape is shown in a different light. My skin still turns brown in the sun. It stretches a little more now when I pinch it, criss-crossed by veins that are becoming prominent with age, a confirmation that blood is indeed going around, that my body is well irrigated, the machine is doing what it does all by itself, as it will until it stops. For the other side to be possible, my blood would have to run backwards beneath that summer-brown skin striated by veins, or else my heart would have to skip a beat. Maybe I went over to the other side and missed my second chance. Maybe I was too busy doing the right thing to take that chance, too busy living like I was supposed to, good girl, firstborn. I'm supposed to do well at everything, and I am not doing well at anything anymore. I can't even pass a pregnancy test that I very much want to fail. I succeed at failing.

Two sides of the same madness. A paper abortion. *Not, not.*

***

Not, not, knot … Once you get going, is there anything else to do other than count them off one at a time like beads on a rosary, praying in spite of yourself, on the altar of your own suffering, in secret, viciously, without believing in it? Not not praying, praying as only those who don't know how to pray can, those who must invent prayer for themselves. Or else those who remain stuck on the first word, who can't get farther than "Our Father." *Not …, not.* Hallowed be whatever. I'm writing in front of a window that faces a church, which I never really saw until I stopped staring at the horizon of words on my screen, both cloistered and boundless. I am doubly enclosed, by the window, transparent and locked, and the church door, locked and impenetrable. There are two screens, too: my eyes, open and unseeing, and my old laptop, open, reflecting what I cannot see. I'm writing about prayer because I can't see the church right in front of me. I am stuttering before its closed doors. *Not, not.*

I'm like Cioran, forever drawn to kneeling like a communicant except I'm holding up my middle finger to the sky. He says it much more elegantly than I do, though; his words have a metaphysical sheen: "Everything in me turns to prayer and blasphemy, everything becomes a call and a refusal."[39] My vital impulse is the same, a coming and going that throws me off balance and makes me homesick, which I worry for you will become wombsickness. How can I spare you the pain, build a bubble around you, give you the world and protect you—from me, my mysticism and resistance, my daily powerlessness and discomfort? I want to shield you and at the same time I want to give you this wreckage of a world that's just as cruel in pieces, the world with which I've struggled, am struggling, and from which I'm increasingly inclined to escape. If I succeed, you will betray me. If you love me, you will betray me.

I can't pray except by writing. It's not really praying: to write is to fight against immediacy by mediation, traces, superimposed ink stains. The page is a palimpsest of the mind layered ever thicker in an attempt to return to a blank page that never existed.

Conversion isn't doing so hot. You—imperial and imperious little woman in my life, your senses thrum with spontaneity as you discover the world. Any form of writing looks like the decadent sophistication of an idle aristocrat by comparison, but I need to go through writing to inhabit the field of your immediacy and be a mother, to be yours. Writing is not a midpoint, the quick stop by the pharmacy on the way home. It's a silly metaphor. I only thought of that because we need TP and nasal spray, but the pharmacy has something Derridean about it. The *pharmakon* is at once remedy and poison, like the double-edged sword of writing. I dream of never having to go to the pharmacy ever again, of having a permanent stash of Tylenol, cough drops, vitamin D, Windex, Kleenex, all of it, my remedies and poisons with me all the time. It never works, it's Sisyphean: you forget something and you have to go back again and again and again.

∗∗∗

Bartleby, Melville's eponymous scribe, is able to free himself through failure; he brilliantly succeeds in evading the world, and also, or most of all, in writing. His only failure concerns the writing of others, which draws him back into writing by reifying him, by making him a figure of thought. His very failure is what makes him a failure, which is almost reassuring.

I would prefer not to. Where syntactically you might expect an infinitive verb to complete the thought, there is nothing. The sentence falls off. "I would prefer not to," Bartleby answers everything requested by his boss, a lawyer puzzled by the phenomenon he has before him, Bartleby's "dead-wall revery"[40] and who is "unmanned,"[41] emasculated; the lawyer is the one who is powerless. Bartleby isn't powerless, he is disarming, unmanning, which is another thing entirely. It's a bit like Heti's "not, not," a negation that contradicts and cancels itself over and over again. The phrase brings us back to Giorgio Agamben's threshold of a negation that preserves its potentiality.[42] It's not Bartleby himself who is not actualized, only the legal documents he is asked to copy. The law is upheld by the text, which can be applied as soon as it is constituted. I've never thought of Bartleby this way, but it came to me today, here in my spot across from the church, that Bartleby is both the heart and the black hole of conversion, a possible turn that is not realized, as Agamben puts it. There is only the stop, a blockage, suspension, subtraction, without any change that might embody what is to come. The balancing point in conversion narratives, which is sometimes pushed aside to get to the catharsis, is held in focus, and it is what gives meaning to the whole narrative, or what is instrumentalized in the structure predicated on the post-conversion point of view, on what will have happened.

It's astounding—the notion of conversion without actualization, conversion at a standstill …

***

What fragments of thought I can pull together have been crumbling for the last three days every time I try to think, a false start every time I have an idea that might allow me to delve into the Bartleby paradox and use it to write something, and which leaves me all alone, stock still on a track going nowhere. Critics have focused exclusively on the character of Bartleby, leaving aside the narrator, the unmanned lawyer who is the mirror in the story, who questions and writes because he doesn't understand, because his lack of understanding emasculates him and reduces him to a powerlessness that he feels is not of the same order as Bartleby's, which is not powerlessness at all. The one who tries to write is the one who comes into contact with true powerlessness.

***

I try to write, free diving beneath the surface of my impotence while you play a version of what Freud called the fort/da, pushing from one end of the apartment to the other on your scooter. You zoom up, say hello, say goodbye, leave again, and it's me who's suffering from your game, I am the one who never wants to lose you, who will inevitably lose you. Our children are borrowed, as the saying goes. Why do I want to write so badly, why do I keep trying? I start pretending to write, just to make your game make sense, since your game at the moment makes more sense than what I'm writing anyway. You see, I need you too, I have to go through you so that my game makes sense, a game that's as crucial as yours. I need to write in order not to desecrate my daily life with you. I need to write because I would rather not wreck everything. I write because I'm scared of wrecking everything, I write because nothing will set me free from writing, especially not writing, writing as an appeal, constant and awkward, to the sacred. I write because I want something to turn over within me. And the more I do it, the more I spread words like peanut butter on the page, until a palimpsestic crust hardens and splits apart, and then maybe I'll be able to slide into a crack, an invisible opening between two words, two letters maybe that have come apart, and disappear there, and there will be nothing else to say after that, the words and sentences will stop unravelling and I will have left it behind, fleeing the word through an inviolate rift that will have opened up com-fuck-ing-pletely at random because clearly I'm not remotely able to construct the arrangement of words required to disappear into a flaw in the sacred.

I no longer know if I'm chasing down conversion, or if conversion is hunting me, hovering at the edges of my mind, never quite taking me in its long, tentacular arms. There must be something wrong with me, something repulsive, like the smell of skunk that wafts in every evening at the same time through the windows open to the deafening din of crickets. Your father wrote to the city to try to get them to come and trap the animal. I can just see some Daniel Boone character with a pelt on his head, tail dangling down, corked cartoon rifle in his hand. The guy at the borough office told him there was no such thing, Monsieur, we don't have trappers, so you'll just have to deal with your own skunk. We could do what they do in the blissful burbs and drown it in a recycling bin. Or just let the unholy stench seep through the world, like cowards.

No one is more annoyed than I am by the daily grind and contingencies of the world. I perform every task helplessly, as if I were being made to dig up corpses with my fingernails or hitchhike in a bikini in Iran. Your mother is a desecrator of the everyday. That's the worst possible thing (apart from infanticidal mothers). How can you pray outside a monastery? How can you write outside a dungeon? You need a prison in order to free yourself from everyday life. As I write, I'm getting up every five minutes to stir my tomato sauce. It is absolutely deranged to live within this kind of contradiction. I am every mother in every generation of my family who cooked each meal and canned every fall so that the family could get through the winter, an allegory of an uncertain, back-breaking, teeth-gritting future. I wince; my tomato sauce is a bit acidic, a bit too spicy too. I am the hysteric unable to scream and begging for refuge. I am the mystic unable to pray and seeking a convent. They're all in there, holding hands and fighting hand to hand, taking on the world as they kill each other. "The state I understand best," Cioran writes, "is desolation which incites prayer but does not go beyond the attempt—what one might call the improbable probability of prayer."[43] Maybe prayer is simply an internalized cry. In Cioran's case, it remains suspended, stretched out along the filament of a life, and it is written because a cry that is not shouted is still a cry, but if it doesn't become prayer it turns into writing or scatters like so many expedients.

**

I alternate between the cemetery and the church as my two writing horizons—two moribund spaces that don't belong to me, that don't contain me, but which keep me in their periphery and therefore also hold me in their sacred axis. This is a sacred barely tethered by the threads of a tradition from which I've largely cut myself loose. And beyond those horizons there is your room, the small, fluffy, luminous cocoon where you pass from rest to awakening and from waking to rest. I keep myself in that sacred axis, too. My office is next door. I can hear you after your nap, singing and chatting with your stuffed animals. You may be a horizon toward which I write, but in fact I write in the shadow of your presence. I write in the interstices. I think of writing as a relationship to space, probably because thought is generally shaped by the tyranny of metaphor. Thought must be represented, illustrated, situated, figured. But it also occurs as a temporality. It's hard to say, because temporality is constraint, time that runs out mechanically and must be made profitable, time compressed between before and after, a hopeless *hic et nunc*. And through it all, writing strives to redeem time. It enacts Benjamin's *Jetztzeit*,[44] the present time, a messianic temporality that opens a breach in the continuum of history and something explodes, something like a frame, a contingency, and with it a vision of a world that is forever shrinking to fit. The relationships between things fall apart and have no time to recreate themselves; thoughts leap out of context. Free thinking, like free diving: if you can hold yourself in the present moment long enough without breathing, the conversion comes out like lungs bursting for air. But then you get up, you go to the bathroom, and there, you've ruined it, you're just breathing again.

***

My sweet little love, all these pages written in secret, in the space between your presence and your needs and I am walking around with my long monkey arms swinging through the world as it slips away from me and where I am slipping away from myself. You are the only thing I don't let go of. If you really did spend your whole life in my arms, maybe I wouldn't have to try to escape, maybe I wouldn't have to try to steal away from you, because you would hold me captive in my own arms. They're long, they can hold you, squeeze you, carry you, and even when you'll be bigger than me, they will be able to hold you still.

I'm walking in the little woodlot by your grandfather's house with you in my arms. You don't want to get down. You're prattling on about the bed of moss beneath our feet, which drinks up every noise except your pretty, tiny, pure voice, the only sound worthy enough not to sink into the marshmallowy green softness of the forest floor. They say it's a sign of a healthy ecosystem. I bury my face in the cloud of your hair. Your little blonde curls bounce against my nose. Your cheeks are even softer than the moss and I kiss them with a string of kisses that is one continuous kiss and I wish it would go on forever as I listen to your mind skip around its associations. Since you've started talking, I have access to that mind, and I understand that the moss makes you think of the texture of the terrycloth bib you wear at daycare, which keeps the splashes and drips at bay when you snack on slices of apple dipped in soy butter. The conversion isn't doing so well right now, my love, but it doesn't really matter. It doesn't matter. You're in my arms, babbling about a world that I tolerate better for your translation of it. Your voice, clear and new, makes the trivial sacred. But I still need to translate the world you're converting into writing—marks on paper like clumps of insect legs, which you don't yet understand—so that I can keep something, hold something in my long arms. When you finally hop down, I am bereft. Just a little longer … Yet when I write, I settle into the loss of motherhood and hide from it in a space that is mute but not deaf, I pour myself into it like water into a crater after the flood.

And I am at a loss for you. Your body cannot be appropriated, it has resisted since mine stopped containing it. My breasts, my arms are incessantly solicited, not because they are mine, but because you need them, and there's Winnicott again sneaking up in another form: there is only good enough, no perfection, no fusion, no absolute, just the day-to-day and its needs, and at the heart of everything, you, my heart, and your unclaimable body, all the months that are now unfurling into years, spent caring for it and loving it, and all time does is pull it farther away from me. Does your mind get closer as your body pulls away? How far from me will your orbit take you? Will my arms always be long enough to touch you? I'm scared sometimes. You see, writing has a way of lodging itself into the slack time of motherhood. That is writing's spot. Like you, when you plop yourself down unceremoniously between my legs as soon as I sit on the floor. Your spot.

***

Writing is lodged in the languor of motherhood and motherhood can only stand alongside writing gone idle. That will be my own shortcoming. There is no conversion without failure.

The game of full and empty is as biological as it is mystical. Breathing, eating, shitting.

Compared to all these normal biological processes, motherhood has that little extra kick of ending on empty. The belly always ends up without a baby, no matter how, no matter how many times. Empty, full, and empty again. Emptiness, fullness, grace, decreation. We never create. I did not create you. I carried you. You come into a state of grace, then you decreate. I don't want to say that being pregnant is a state of grace—no way, at least not in the image of the beaming fertility goddess contentedly caressing her swollen belly; it's more beat-up than beatific, roiling hormones battered by lack of alcohol. It's weary; a weary grace, let's say. Now I'm empty again and I don't know what I'm waiting for. My stomach is flat. My ribs stick out a little. You once tried to grab onto my collarbones. You know empty when you can hold on to the bones. And you're just supposed to leave it there, you're not supposed to struggle, there are no stopgaps. Give it up, throw it all up. But I have a phobia of vomit. I'm not ready for any sacrifice that will affect you, and I'm no maternal martyr either. Being your mother is decreating the illusion of possessing you, though I do want to be able to own your kisses forever, your small, wet, scrumptious pink strawberry that reaches out and offers me, yes, a moment of grace, landing on my face with a small, almost inaudible smack, and then it disappears in the blink of an eye.

***

Sublime asceticism is not within my reach. I suffer, badly and in secret, in the gaps between your needs. You are the obstacle to my suffering in circles, a bottomless asceticism, the whirlpool that would suck up my ego and wait for God to fish me out like a soggy rag from a well. There's nothing especially mystical about motherhood, I think—just two words carried along together by weak alliteration. Despite everything, as soon as the spot facing the church is free, I grab my notebooks, my computer, and my bag and I sneak over, ass in chair. It's superstition; I'm a parasite feeding slyly on what I am not entitled to. As if by my looking at it, the door would suddenly open wide on a sacred all-you-can-eat buffet. "Waiting and suffering," Simone Weil laments, "we are now before the gate":

> If we must, we will break it open
> with our blows.
> We press and we push, but we cannot
> shift its weight.
> We must languish, be patient and
> watch in vain.

We look upon the gate, shut fast,

unbreakable.[45]

Kafka's characters lamented before doors too.[46] It is the great allegory of our relationship to the sacred in the last century. To be honest, who knows what I would do if the door actually opened, just like that, without my having knocked. Would I go in? Would I hide? Would I watch it open along the thin, myopic slit above my glasses, my eyes squinting at the screen, and keep on typing? Contemplating a closed door reconciles me with divine withdrawal in some way.

I would like to surrender to something that is not paid for with grace. Weil fled from everything that was gratifying, she descended into a "state of extreme and total humiliation"[47] and clung to it, was granted grace. But asceticism, suffering, and humiliation are the purview and the joy of saints and madwomen. Don't tell me Simone wasn't sated, at the end; physical starvation was spiritual nourishment. I'm not talking about masochism; I think if she had to choose, she would have fallen on the side of sadism. You know you can't have both. Weil lived in a world of gratification, where everything she did to herself physically was returned to her spiritually. It's the first abandonment that hurts, and after that you reap. More than Saint Simone I think I'll take Kerouac, a constipated angel complaining up on his cloud, on his way to heaven but stalled halfway up—constipation is heavy—and contemplating the rest of the infinite sky because the higher you go, the more sky there is—while weeping in Canuck, a language made for lamenting. "My witness is the empty sky," he moans in *Some of the Dharma*.[48] When I say that I would like to surrender to what is not paid in grace—what a crock of shit that is. It would mean surrendering to immanence without verticality, and yet I write, telling myself that I might find some leverage in this jumble of letters. But if conversion is decreation, where do I find the point of grace between the letters I align and those I erase? Should I hit delete all the way back to the beginning, keep only the title and after that a sheaf of bound white sheets?

To erase would be to deny my escape, which has become as vital to me as your presence. To erase, strangely enough, would be the opposite of decreation.

***

In Greek mythology, the seasons come from a daughter who has escaped her mother. Or else from a mother who wouldn't accept that her daughter might escape. Watching you run toward me, waiting for you, a few seconds and my arms close around you and you're holding on to me too, though not for long, I know, you'll have another, much more exciting project soon enough, and this feeling of passing fullness, a few seconds when I'm carrying all your weight, your legs and arms wrapped around me, and I can bury my nose in your neck and breathe in that smell I never want to lose. Empty, full, and empty once more and I have to fill up again because I'll break down otherwise. The body is like the seasons—empty, full, empty again, full again, until the final winter. You are no longer my fullness. You are outside my body. Next to me. You are no longer my absolute immersion in a fullness that enveloped me in softness, kisses, cries, tears, yours, mine, intertwined, and which sometimes suffocated me. You can run now, and you love to run, so you're no longer my captive. When I go for a run, it's a predictable loop, ten kilometres from you to you. It's fall now, and the cycle of the seasons has come between us. As you create yourself, I must decreate the Demeter into which I have converted. I can't do it; I will try. I don't know if I will, and if I should, or not.

***

No. No, I think I'll try not to.

My grandmother died last night, the one who was nobody to you because I wanted it that way. The one who personified the scent of aggression mothers hold, mothers who swing from the grace of the Madonna to infanticide in a snap, a burp, a howl. Did the spectre of the bad mother I carry with me, which over time took on her sharp edges and the rattle of her voice, did that shadow die with her? We'll have to go to the funeral. For my mother, your grandmother.

As a child, I hated it when we went to that village, its stink of secrecy and death. For twenty-five years, I didn't go back. Now what? Do I return, armed with my love for you? Do I run after you in the empty church of a village that already smelled like death twenty-five years ago, only to realize in a throbbing flash of anguish that this place is not meant for you, we have to get out of there right now, rewind, go back, run back down the stairs and slam the door, take off, tires screeching, and hold our breath for a hundred kilometres, spit out the dusty black seclusion once we're on the highway, just far enough away from the zombies. To have gone that far. And for once the church doors were open!

The place is haunted and everybody knows it. There's nothing we can do about it. We just have to get out of there. I'd like us to find an island and for the three of us to be our own origin story, just that, a beginning, love degree zero, without the twisted heritage of transmission, without the ghosts. Is that too much to ask? Stay with me, run away with me, my love. I have to betray something that is the opposite of you: where I come from. I have to tear my hair out, my skin, so that you're not like us, all tangled up like hair caught in the same ancestral chewing gum. An island, ghosts, zombies and bubble gum. Metaphors are never too dispassionate when you want to make good your escape, leave, say no to everything, even to the dead.

I'm not going back. I'll stay away, armed with my love for you. Hades is no place for you, my daughter, you're staying with me.

∗∗∗

Now that I have you, that I ran away with you, that I fed you with my flesh and then with my scars, that I finally recognize myself in this hybrid figure of Demeter and Persephone, who are one, mother–daughter–mother, entwined like the tentacles of a jellyfish, a knotted snake biting its own tail, I can stop hyperventilating and let the writing catch its breath.

I feel that I am nearing an end. As usual, I'll probably stop for a few moments before I land.

It will be an ending that isn't one, an ending you ponder, unsure, your eyes tired of trying to keep up with the ping-pong of conversion. I'm not sure what makes this an ending; I haven't reached any kind of conclusion. Am I giving up too quickly? Did I want to postpone my conversion as much as I wanted to achieve it? Is it there, right in front of me but too murky or not bright enough for me to see it again, or ever? I'm waiting for a messiah to appear out of the squalor of fire that spews out the ass end of a shuttle, but all I see are the fireflies. There are fireflies. My conversion is dimly lit because it is wild, as sacred as it is ambiguous.

And in this place and time, on November 15, 2019, on this page, sitting at my desk, the right side of my body aching from an early winter squall, I raise my head and contemplate the damage, all the disquieting strangeness of writing, its magic and its holy horror, spread out before me: the remnants know more than the author who wrought them. I could end up like that. I've never known how to end. I don't want this story to end. I'm afraid of emptiness.

Sitting in my office, a few hiccups away from an ending, and I can't tell what this is in front of me. I like the idea of having a thinking cave, like Thomas Bernhard. I commandeered a big room in our apartment, my writing cell. Except I never close the door, so it's not much good as a dungeon. It breaks my heart to think of little Rachel Zucker standing in front of the closed door of her mother's workroom: "I remember so little but can recall in vivid detail the way the outside of the office door of her study felt beneath my small palm as I stood, listening, trying to decide whether to knock, whether to risk her wrath by interrupting."[49]

I've never liked living in a world of closed doors. No closed door can keep you out anyway; I can never even pee in peace. You amble into my very minimum-security writing prison whenever you want—to play ball with me, eat your pistachios and leave the shells all over the place, make me read you a story in the blue easy chair. To usurp my place, sit at my desk, spill your glass of milk and play in the puddle. Maybe writing among your pistachio shells, as if you'd left them there so I won't get lost, glancing at a doll sprawled across your fire engine, is enough to absolve me.

***

I want Dufourmantelle to tell me again that I don't need absolution, I want to rediscover my tearful relief when I read the last pages of *La femme et le sacrifice* a few months ago.

> Why have so many women perceived writing as antagonistic to family life, to life itself, or why have they negotiated it badly, painfully, with difficulty? Neurotic logic always wants us to give up. As if we could not be devoted to a book and to a child at the same time, as if they were opposites. A child asks for nothing more than love and attention, but certainly not sacrifice, for which they would have to pay a double price—their mother's and their own. A creative mother is not entirely theirs, nor is she entirely there. A part of her is elsewhere, summoned to listen to the voices she herself has called forth in her work, and the child also receives this absence as a gift, since they then participate, in their own way, in this other space to which they feel their mother is being summoned and to which they too wish to turn. The woman who believes she is sacrificing herself for her child is in truth sacrificing herself for something else entirely; another kind of tyranny, one that is far more implacable.[50]

This space and this time I have stolen from you—here, it's yours. It's not the remnants I'm giving you, those are for others; the book of leavings is addressed to whoever will read it so you don't have to. What I'm giving you is desire tucked into escape, the call of something else—a transcendence that, though it lifts me off the ground now and again, it never takes me away from the closeness and sanctity of us. You allowed me to find a self freed from its own ventriloquism, no longer fumbling around in criticism. The scar has been traced. You have turned me into a writer. In writing, I have felt the contours of my new shape as a mother—the same as before your stay in my womb, only sharper. Writing has converted me into a mother. I don't know if I'll experience another conversion. It doesn't matter. It doesn't matter at all.

Notes

1. Anne Dufourmantelle, *La sauvagerie maternelle* (Paris: Calmann-Lévy, 2001), 24. Excerpts translated by Katia Grubisic.

2. Rachel Zucker, "Diary [Persephone]," in *Eating in the Underworld* (Middletown, CT: Wesleyan University Press, 2015), 5.

3. Rachel Zucker, *MOTHERs* (Denver: Counterpath Press, 2013), 110–111.

4. Dufourmantelle, *La sauvagerie maternelle*, 19.

5. Maggie Nelson, *The Argonauts* (Minneapolis: Graywolf Press, 2015), 155–156.

6. Dufourmantelle, *La sauvagerie maternelle*, 19.

7. Dufourmantelle, *La sauvagerie maternelle*, 28.

8. Zucker, *MOTHERs*, 111.

9. Emil Cioran, *Cahiers 1958–1972* (Paris: Gallimard, 1997). Excerpts translated by Katia Grubisic.

10. Michel Foucault, *"L'écriture de soi,"* Corps écrit 5 (February 1983 [L'Autoportrait]): 3–23.

11. Pierre Hadot, *Exercices spirituels et philosophie antique* (Paris: Albin Michel, 2003), 223. Excerpt translated by Katia Grubisic.

12. Mathieu Riboulet, *Entre les deux il n'y a rien* (Paris: Verdier, 2015), 12. Excerpt translated by Katia Grubisic.

13. Alice Notley, "A Baby is Born Out of a White Owl's Forehead," in *Mysteries of Small Houses: Poems* (New York: Penguin Poets, 1998), 38–39.

14. Rudolf Otto, *The Idea of the Holy*, trans. John W. Harvey (London: Galaxy Books – Oxford University Press, 1958).

15. D. W. Winnicott, *Playing and Reality* (London: Tavistock Publications, 1971).

16. Rachel Cusk, *A Life's Work: On Becoming a Mother* (New York: Picador, 2015), 80.

17. Cusk, *A Life's Work*, 80–81.

18. Annie Dillard, *The Writing Life* (New York: Harper Perennial, 1990), 12–13.

19. Knut Hamsun, *Hunger*, trans. George Egerton (Delhi: Lector House, 2019).

20. Thomas Bernhard, *The Lime Works*, trans. Sophie Wilkins (New York: Vintage International, 2010), 164.

21. Dillard, *The Writing Life*, 20.

22. Clarice Lispector, "The Egg and the Chicken," in *The Complete Stories*, trans. Katrina Dodson (New York: New Directions, 2015), 280.

23. Lispector, "The Egg and the Chicken," 286.

24. Lispector, "The Egg and the Chicken," 278.

25. Lispector, "The Egg and the Chicken," 279.

26. Sheila Heti, *Motherhood* (Toronto: Alfred A. Knopf, 2018), 21.

27. Heti, *Motherhood*, "A Further Note."

28. Heti, *Motherhood*, 193.

29. Heti, *Motherhood*, 187.

30. Heti, *Motherhood*, 257.

31. Heti, *Motherhood*, 162.

32. Zucker, *MOTHERs*, 31.

33. Patti Smith, *Devotion* (New Haven: Yale University Press, 2017), 13.

34. Heti, *Motherhood*, 157.

35. Heti, *Motherhood*, 157.

36. Heti, *Motherhood*, 157–158.

37. Saint Augustine of Hippo, *The Confessions*, trans. Maria Boulding (San Francisco: Ignatius Press, 1996), 206.

38. Søren Kierkegaard, *Repetition and Philosophical Crumbs*, trans. Marilyn Gaye

Piety (Oxford: Oxford University Press, 2009).

39. Cioran, *Cahiers 1958–1972*, 13.

40. Herman Melville, "Bartleby the Scrivener: A Story of Wall-Street," in *Essential Stories* (Hanover, NH: Steerforth Press, 2021), 46.

41. Melville, "Bartleby the Scrivener," 36.

42. Giorgio Agamben, "Bartleby, or On Contingency," in *Potentialities: Collected Essays in Philosophy*, trans. Daniel Heller-Roazen (Redwood City, CA: Stanford University Press, 1999).

43. Cioran, *Cahiers 1958–1972*, 320.

44. See Walter Benjamin, "Theses on the Philosophy of History," in *Illuminations: Essays and Reflections*, trans. Harry Zohn (New York: Schocken, 1968).

45. Simone Weil, "The Gate," in *Gateway to God*, trans. Paul Keegan (Glasgow: Fontana – Collins, 1974), 15.

46. See notably Franz Kafka, *The Trial*, trans. Idris Parry (Penguin, 2012).

47. Simone Weil, "Human Personality," in *Simone Weil: Selected Essays 1934–1943*, trans. Richard Rees (Eugene, OR: Wipf and Stock, 1986), 27.

48. Jack Kerouac, *Some of the Dharma* (New York: Penguin, 1997), 221.

49. Zucker, *MOTHERs*, 122.

50. Anne Dufourmantelle, *La femme et le sacrifice: D'Antigone à la femme d'à côté* (Paris: Denoël, 2007), 332–333. Excerpt translated by Katia Grubisic.

Author Sara Danièle Michaud holds a doctorate in comparative literature from the Université de Montréal and pursued postdoctoral work on conversion narratives at the University of Toronto. Her research and publications have often looked at the notion of the sacred and the intersection of philosophy and literature. She currently teaches literature at the Cégep de Saint-Laurent. Her fourth book, *Cicatrices, Carnets de conversion* (Nota Bene, 2022) was shortlisted for the Prix des libraires 2023.

Katia Grubisic is a writer, editor, and translator whose work has appeared in various Canadian and international publications. Her collection *What if red ran out* (Goose Lane Editions, 2008) was shortlisted for the A.M. Klein Prize for Poetry and won the 2009 Gerald Lampert award for best first book. Her translations of David Clerson's first novel, *Brothers* (QC Fiction, 2016) and of *A Cemetery for Bees*, by Alina Dumitrescu (LLP 2020), were shortlisted for the Governor General's Award.

Singles Essays

Scar Tissue: Tracing Motherhood is the most recent in a series of short Singles essays in English and in French by distinguished Canadian writers and translators on a wide range of topics of contemporary and abiding interest.

Linda Leith Publishing | Linda Leith Éditions.

Black Community Resource Centre. **Where They Stood: The Evolution of the Black Anglo Community in Montreal.** LLP, 2023. ISBN: 9781773901343.

Boullata, Issa J. **The Bells of Memory: A Palestinian Boyhood in Jerusalem**. LLP, 2014. ISBN: 9781927535394.

Deguire, Eric. **Communication et violence. Des récits personnels à l'hégémonie américaine,** essai. LLÉ, 2020. ISBN: 9781773900605.

Delvaux, Martine. **Nan Goldin: The Warrior Medusa**, trans. David Homel. LLP, 2017. ISBN: 9781988130552.

Drimonis, Toula. **We, the Others: Allophones, Immigration, and Belonging in Canada**. LLP, 2022. ISBN: 9781773901213.

Farman, Abou. **Clerks of the Passage**. LLP, 2012. ISBN: 9780987831743.

Farman Abou. **Les lieux de passage, essais sur le mouvement et la migration,** trad. Marianne Champagne. LLÉ, 2016. ISBN : 9781988130200.

Fletcher, Raquel. **Who Belongs in Quebec? Identity Politics in a Changing Society.** LLP, 2020. ISBN: 9781927535394.

Gollner, Adam Leith. **Working in the Bathtub: Conversations with the Immortal Dany Laferrière**. LLP 2021. ISBN: 9781773900735.

Henighan, Stephen. **A Green Reef: The Impact of Climate Change**. LLP, 2013. ISBN: 9781927535271.

Jedwab, Jack. **Counterterrorism and Identities: Canadian Viewpoints**. LLP 2015. ISBN. 9781927535868.

Lavoie, Frédérick. **For Want of a Fir Tree: Ukraine Undone**, trans. Donald Winkler. LLP, 2018. ISBN: 97819881305934.

Michaud, Sara Danièle. **Scar Tissue: Tracing Motherhood**, trans. Katia Grubisic. LLP 2023. ISBN: 9781773901374.

Navarro, Pascale. **Women and Power: The Case for Parity**, trans. David Homel. LLP 2016. ISBN 9781988130156

Péan, Stanley. **Taximan**, trans. David Homel. LLP 2018. ISBN: 9781988130897.

Rowland, Wade. **Saving the CBC: Balancing Profit and Public Service**. LLP, 2013. ISBN: 9781927535110.

Rowland, Wade. **Canada Lives Here: The Case for Public Broadcasting**. LLP 2015. ISBN: 9781927535820.

Salutin, Rick. **Keeping the Public in Public Education**. LLP, 2012. ISBN: 9780987831729.

MIX
Paper from
responsible sources
FSC® C100212

Printed by Imprimerie Gauvin
Gatineau, Québec